University of South Florida Press / Tampa

Testimony

SELECTED POEMS, 1954–1986

Hans Juergensen

The publication costs of this book were underwritten by a grant from the University of South Florida Research Council.

UNIVERSITY PRESSES OF FLORIDA is the central agency for scholarly publishing of the State of Florida's university system, producing books selected for publication by the faculty editorial committees of Florida's nine public universities: Florida A&M University (Tallahassee), Florida Atlantic University (Boca Raton), Florida International University (Miami), Florida State University (Tallahassee), University of Central Florida (Orlando), University of Florida (Gainesville), University of North Florida (Jacksonville), University of South Florida (Tampa), University of West Florida (Pensacola).

ORDERS for books published by all member presses should be addressed to University Presses of Florida, 15 NW 15th Street, Gainesville, FL 32603.

Library of Congress Cataloging-in-Publication Data

Juergensen, Hans, 1919–
    Testimony : selected poems, 1954–1986.

    I. Title.
PS3519.U445T48   1989   811'.54   88-33789
ISBN 0-8130-0916-2

FOR MY FAMILY

Ilse

Claudia and Hector

Andy and Nathan

Contents

Acknowledgments IX
Testimony 1

1. IN THE BEGINNING

Untitled 6
The Circumstance 8
Sempiternal 10
David 11
Amos 17
A Parable 20
Isaiah 22
Jeremiah 24
An Epilogue by Baruch, the Disciple of Jeremiah 27

2. SHEOL

Inscription 31
De Facto 32
The Scar—August, 1934 33
Holocaust 35
Ballad 36
Bars of Dust 38
Too Everywhere 39
Response to a Grand Inquisitor 40
Grisha's Epilogue 42
Ultimate Recall 44
Untitled 45
Forty Years after Liberation 47

3. IRONIES

Genesis 37—New Edition 51
Sectarians 53

Anathema 54
Fragment, Dating Back to the Dark Ages 55
York, A.D. 1189 57
Had They Been There 59
Sermon from the Ammunition Hatch
of the Ship of Fools 60
Miserabile 61

4. WITNESS

Preface 65
Maimonides 66
Spinoza 67
Franz Kafka 68
Albert Camus 69
Refugee Memoir 70
Journey to Orcus 71
Nelly Sachs 73
April 5, 1968—Martin Luther King 74
Lament for Paul Celan (1920–1970) 75
Pablo Neruda 77
"The Gates of the Forest" 78
Encounter 79

5. RESURGENCE

Summary 83
Anniversary—October, 1965 85
Hasidic Dance 86
The Denmark Square Monument in Jerusalem 87
Memorandum 88
The Chagall Windows 90
Chai 91

6. TRANSLATIONS FROM NELLY SACHS'S
JOURNEY INTO A DUSTLESS REALM

Acknowledgments

Many of the poems in this collection have appeared in the following books by the author: *I Feed You From My Cup* (Hamden, Conn.: Quinnipiac College, 1958); *In Need for Names* (Baltimore: Linden Press, 1960); *Existential Canon* (Fort Smith, Ark.: South and West, 1965); *Sermons from the Ammunition Hatch of the Ship of Fools* (New Orleans: Vagabond Press, 1968); *from the divide* (Homestead, Fla.: Olivant Press, 1970); *Hebraic Modes* (Homestead, Fla.: Olivant Press, 1972); *Journey toward the Roots* (St. Petersburg, Fla.: Valkyrie Press, 1976); *Fire-Tested* (Bourbonnais, Ill.: Lieb-Schott Publications, 1983).

The following poems appeared previously in these periodicals: "The Circumstance," *Confrontation* (Florida Hillel Foundation, Spring 1978); "Holocaust," *UT Review*, Tampa University (1975); "Genesis, 37—New Edition," *Impact 1*, no. 2 (1974); "Fragment, Dating Back to the Dark Ages," *Impact 2*, no. 7 (1975); "Miserabile," *South and West* (Fall 1978); "Journey to Orcus," *Weid*, no. 51 (1977); "Pablo Neruda," in *For Neruda for Chile*, ed. Walter Lowenfels (Boston: Beacon Press, 1975); "No Kaddish Was Said," in *Report of the National Holocaust Conference* (Philadelphia, 1979); "Had They Been There," *Kindred Spirit* (Winter 1987).

Testimony

The sun rises
         we say
And steeps the east
In that peculiar glow
No painter dares
         Therefore what can you name it
         Except another day

Having watched my number
         Of these
i would like to shrug
         But cannot
         While that hawk is gliding
         His hunting circles
         Black black
         Against the retina

         As a totem of destiny
         Unto some creature
         Which also stirs
         Along its feeding trail

Theirs the dynamics
Of Nature's nature
Across the rooted facets
Of Wordsworthian reminiscence
Blanked into shiny verse
         Yet too deceptive
         To deceive

         For this planet's crust
         Is stretched too thin
         To awe us longer

         Us the volatile
         Parodists

                    Under a wisdom
                    Nibbling at apogees

How do i know such truths
How verify frustration
i the image cutter
The word combiner
The predatory explicator
Of hawk
Of rabbit
Of utter space . . .

But i have listened to Mahler
Who scored the edge of things
By heaving cubes of pathos
Into place
Then mortar-sealing them
With gallows jests
Though asking
(Childlike)
                    What is this block
                    With the blotched groove
                    And why that axe

                    Then lighting up
                    (Childlike once more)
                    Because the lore of
                                        misery
                    Sounds so exciting

Since all those men of strength
Were executed when the sun rose up

                    The sun again
                    The hawk again
                    This time himself
                    The hunted

The days
          Then
Starting from the sun
Meeting the east of
My horizon
Sting like pebbles
Trapped in a shoe
Never to be cast off

never to be cast off

1. In the Beginning

I

God blew across his palm,
light sparked forth,
infinity-aimed.
but some imperfection
splintered purity.

the Word,
like a paternal finger,
pointed at the essence:

ONE

yet the flames of creation
were henceforth tainted
by two-fold hues:

light had acquired
shadows.

II

space the brain pan of God:

every galaxy a predicate
bearing through
the infinite syntax.

naive reduction
of the laboriously
discerned
   . . . by horn-rimmed
seekers after facts
folded in formulae;

scored nonetheless
as trickling grains
in rills
of the perpetual.

III

In his depraved universe
he that was of the light
slithers through degradation
on sand-biting scales.

Even now he startles us
with attenuated beauty
despite venomed stealth
or lidless stare.

When he strikes
it is in cold-blooded dread
of eternal revenge.

The Circumstance

Flames gyre about that bush!

The exile's eyes need shielding
from so much miracle.

Those grueling crags demand
shod soles—
although a voice insists:
"Remove your sandals, Moses."

Enveloped in man-Onlyness
before that Singularity,
he does not suffer
from searing stone.

With churning blood
he listens
to inchoate twistings
of his own untutored tongue;
and—in a blazing trance—
stammers submission.

I-AM is wrapped in silence.

—Now to retrace himself
through tracklessness to Goshen,
and then impel a shall-be nation
from servile safety
toward these peaks of LAW!

. . . Ready to thong
his sandals
upon scarred feet,
he dares to raise his lids:

the God-struck bush
stands—once again—
a bush.

Sempiternal

Silence
        haunched silence
Job
   inscrutable victor

Done with
           cursing and mourning
Emptied
      like a wine skin
      of his ferment
Scratching indignities
     with an absence of mind
     worthy of a cur

Ashes on pustulant lips
                neither trembling
Nor sneering
      even at righteous leeches
Only alive
    the nub of a wager
Exhausting
     Satan and Yahveh

   Transfigured

   Icon enduring
   Haunched silence

David

His lyre hangs upon its peg
nearly unstrung.
Age has loosened
the instrument,
the song;
and David's blood
spreads slower
everyday
so that the newest concubine
can warm it
rarely now,
however lithely
she applies her art.

Like Saul
before him,
he broods—counting
sentinels
along the ramparts—
hammering
Nathan's anathemas,
phrase by phrase,
upon the anvil
of his brain.

A somnolent
Jerusalem
roots at his feet;
its dimmer stirrings
in his awareness,
though unheard.

Of all he comprehends
little has ripened truth.

The ghosts he made
dangle before his eye
like Absalom
whose hair soughs
through the groves . . .

. . . Nathan had
warned him
that this was to be:
Bathsheba's lust,
sealed with
Uriah's courage,
bore him the name
of Peace
but not the fruit.

                .   .   .   .   .

Not much is left
of night,
not much
of life.
His fingers
cannot grip
a well-turned hilt
as once they did.

"O bones, my bones
beneath
this scabrous skin—
how brittle rings
the iron of your past!"

. . . the past—
it seeps up
from the sands
of afterthought
like cistern freshets:
      Hue and Cry:

Battle and Pestilence:
Faith and Defection.

First sling,
then scepter,
shield and sword—
and always
Nathan
with his shofar blast:
    "Fear ye the Lord!
    Be righteous . . . "

David smiles.
Gently, his heart-throat
chants
those meters
Adonai imposed
and he fulfilled:
                imperfectly,
with wildly stumbling feet
and avaricious fists,
yet sore intent
upon the law.

Justice
is hard to come by
for mere mortals,
in spite of
hoary tablets—
wherefore he sang
his thoughts
often . . .

Selah.
The rhapsodies
are quelled.
The mountains,
whence came help,
now lean

like threats
forever to be guarded.

Only that valley
of the shadow,
where Jonathan
had feared
and judged his heart,
stretches—
                    a sea
no captain
may assuage.

"Prophet,"
the monarch murmurs,
"I am but a man,
a warrior chief
with needs
beyond recall.
I love my people,
and I love my God:
and power, too,
and thighs
about my loins . . . "

                .   .   .   .   .

The Ark, he knows,
rests somewhere
in his dreams.
Its sacred care
remains his purest task:
balm for transgressions,
oil to lave the soul.
"I shall," he vows,
"give it a golden house!"

    . . . and sighs,
from out the depth,

against the crown
for having scattered years
like panicked sheep.

.   .   .   .   .

Will they live?
Outstand perhaps
the citadel,
the throne,
the dynasty—
the grievances of God?

.   .   .   .   .

He rises slowly
to the clank
of commandeered relief.
Another dark trickles its stars
from everlastingness
to everlasting—
his chilly carcass
watching . . .

But he is King
and poet.
And he firms
his step to young resolve;
takes down
the idle harp
tightens its gut
and—oblivious
to pitch—
spawns lines
once more
into the dawn
of time:

"The Lord is gracious
   and merciful

Slow to anger and abounding
in steadfast love . . . "

This much is sure.
This much has
never changed.

David endures
this joy—
that tensile words
have bloomed
to understanding:

God's Name,
he feels,
is spoken sound;
but the reality
is cosmic grace . . . .

This poem received the Stephen Vincent Benét Award for 1970.

Amos

O Nabi, you rise before me
in the shepherd's garment,
redolent of shaggy rams—
the knotted crook
clutched like a spear
in your fist.

Multitudes mill through the gate
of Beth-El, pursuing their purpose
according to their station—
portly or haggard—
each girdled by vanity.

Many direct leery glances
at you;
then lower their eyes
and furtively snake away
to search out a milder face.

Some, of sufficient desire,
listen for apt quotations
issued by this new prophet—
delusive, for all they know . . .

A hard core crowds about you—
fear clawing its viscera—
to hear and weigh the anger
they dare not give tongue of their own.

Noon-white, the city's ramparts
din with the barter
in goods,
in beasts,
in gods
and men:

Justice does *not* roll like water,
nor Righteousness like a mighty stream.

Those walls will be razed.
Their dust shall augment the desert;
For—whence, in this arid season,
    shall waters roll? . . .

    The words from your lips
    sow no seeds.
    The afflicted, encircling you,
    clench their teeth over impotence.
    And the children, open-mouthed,
    cannot yet comprehend
    that it shall be *their* fate
    your parallels hammer out,
    while bleating creatures are trussed
    to be drained under priestly knives
    for the tittle of their Law.

    But God despises the stench
    and spews out
    these prayed-over morsels,
    these steaming formulas.—

Denied and reviled,
o Amos,
you turn south,
toward your hut in Tekoah
and badger YAWEH,
who commands you back to the north.

You obey.
You continue your task—
and the people again cast you out.

Nothing is left to do
save the written outcry of harshness,
your brethren's degradation.

Yet:
that scroll will also record
that the Lord must cleave
to His Pledge
and spare a Remnant,
in His mysterious mercy—
un-merited perhaps,

but fire-tested!

A Parable

Having seen vines shrivel
and thorns snaring
the sumptuous robes
of Ephraim,
Hosea suspected that God
meant to punish
Israel's digressions;

for the chosen one
whored after deities
not amenable to the Lord,
and grew stout
from the traffic
with Baal's brazen subjects.

Therefore,
Jehovah charged His servant
to take unto himself
a harlot
and to beget three children.

and HE saw to it
that said harlot
would betray said servant
by hiring herself out
to more affluent lovers.

        .   .   .   .   .

Now, it is written
that Hosea loved this woman
and took her back
whenever she repented.

        .   .   .   .   .

The prophet, then,
enumerated
God's grievances
against Ephraim, Jacob
and even Judah
in stirring rhetoric,
pronouncing dire results
for the Northern Kingdom,
while—for the time being—
excusing the Southern one.

. . . . .

There existed an obvious gap
in the communication
between the divine
and the merely human parties.

The consequences proved cruel.

. . . . .

But:
flickering among the threats
shone a brief flame
of compassion.

Hosea's heart was forgiving;
and, eventually, God approved . . . .

Isaiah

ZION, the Lord's beloved,
is a virgin no more.

She lusts after Edom's abominations
and Egypt's unguents,
not heeding the cloying venom
that defiles her prurient blood.

.   .   .   .   .

Vociferous greed swelters
along her thoroughfares,
outbidding the eddying sighs
of tattered desperation.

Cant and Arrogance gather
their aromatic raiment about them,
recoiling with dainty distaste
from Jacob's malodorous descendants,
whose simple manhood and pride
they have savaged for generations.

Warriors jangle
through teeming alleys
in search of flesh-confrontations
before *their* tomorrows
of carnage.

.   .   .   .   .

The city seethes
like a molten stream;
but the late, blesséd groves
lie vulture-stripped:
rank valleys of bleaching bones . . .

For Jehovah remains incensed
and has withdrawn His hand
from that daughter
adjudged a harlot.

.   .   .   .   .

No prophet can stay the verdict.

Even the noblest
of inspired tacticians—
who, for forty graying years,
warded off conquering hordes—
even *he* cannot divert
the shattering sentence.
Albeit,
with a last glorious resolve,
his vision ascends
to a great new song
of indivisible faith;

and he proclaims
that Judah's saving remnant
shall teach the
ONENESS of GOD
to all the nations,
and stand tall
in redemptive holiness.

Jeremiah

With ashes upon my head
and a yoke about my shoulders
I showed myself in the streets
of Zion's daughter—
suffering between
the Lord's wrath
and the fury of the patriots.

Mine was the
irresistible urge
of God's command.

> "Go unto my people,"
> He said.
> "Restrain their
> warlike preparations.

> "Their alliances
> shall not avail,
> for I have
> delivered them
> unto the sword
> of Babylon."

So spoke the Lord.

I remonstrated with Him,
like Moses,
since my tongue
was equally locked,
and I had not the words.

But who can prevail
against The Name?

. . . . .

The cauldron from the north
tilted toward Jerusalem.

And I was branded a traitor . . .

and was cast
into a pit,
there to perish
in my wrong-headedness
like Joseph,
though my sin
was not vanity;
nor did I preen myself
with star-dreams
in which I shone
as the sun-like center.

The King pitied my misery
and ordered me freed
from the mire.

I could have bought peace
with silence.
But God left me
no choice.

.   .   .   .   .

My days are painfully long;
they weigh heavy upon me.

.   .   .   .   .

Chaldaea sheltered me
with honor;
but there, too,
I grew wearisome
—to host and exile—
with my lamentations.

I found no surcease.

HE goaded my spirit
into harping speech—
from the gate of Ishtar
to the banks of the Nile.

. . . . .

I know that my countrymen
will stone me to death,
and shall welcome
the release.

. . . . .

But the Holy One
has made me
His partner
and kindled a flame
within my soul
that must burn
forever.

Now,
I am of Him,
and HE is of me;
and the children
of dispersion
will know
HIM
as the
LOVING MYSTERY
in their yearning
heart of hearts.

An Epilogue by Baruch, the Disciple of Jeremiah

Induced by an irate Deity
through the stammering of my teacher
to me,
blood-chilling images
darkened the scrolls,
stinging as thistles.

Thus I became
the scribe of woe,
terrified by the scratchings
of my hesitant quill.

He, whose writhing shadow
paced up and down
before me into anathema dawns,
could never smile—
he saw only sin and its wages.

And I found no time to weep—
not for him,
nor my people,
nor myself—
his visions were too demanding.

. . . . .

Now that he has achieved
peace,
my days approach and depart
in bitter desolation.

I have no home, no kin.

. . . . .

. . . Why did the Omnipotent
visit destruction upon us
without a winnowing?

And:
will those forebodings
I recorded
alter the human flaw?

. . . . .

Like them,
too insignificant for exile,
I eke out a stony existence
among these unyielding hills
and have merely salvaged
my life.

Yet, I need to seek God again
within my own presence—
although He has receded
into the unknown
and will not speak to me.

Still: I am of His creation
and—at unhoped-for hours,
enraptured by its wonders
or the simplest act of kindness—

and that, perhaps,
must suffice.

2. Sheol

Inscription

At times my
veins burn in
defiance of the civilized.

Whoever has
heard bones
snap or voices
twist,

Knows
what
I
mean.

De Facto

smoke curtains the pit:
for the fraction of
a startled throb
only, i glimpse
blackened bones,

i knew they were there:
jeanne d'arc,
huss, lattimer—
courageous strangers
who,
even the best of
their kind,
had equally consigned
my ancestors.

but i do not turn away
i have pity
still,
for i too
know the proximity
of flames,
and

under my skin
and muscle
hinge
bones like
theirs.

The Scar—August, 1934

The clearing ahead shimmered
In the wealth of August
When summer hangs heaviest
In the branches.
The trail's moss yielded
Underfoot; everywhere emerald
With a mere edge of rose.

This I recall seeing,
As my older friend and I
Walked those uneasy steps,
Aware of being stalked.
Boots crackled through decay
Hardened in Prussian seasons.
We dared not speak.

The black tunics felt sinister:
Their holstered purpose moved
Sure, well trained . . .
My friend and I were Jews.

The clearing smelled
of mown grass,
Acid-sweet—
The afternoon had
Almost stopped.
My friend's head inclined
Fate flecked his eyes.—
I meant to run.—
But we decided
To face fear instead.

. . . a sharpness of flame
Spewed toward me.
One black arm jerked back
With the report I never heard:
It was my friend who died.

He lay face down.
I waited for my moment—
No longer quite afraid,
Or making thoughts.
The executioner approached
Unhurried—not unkindly—
Weapon slack, to warn:

> "Sag' nichts davon;   "You understand
> Sonst weisst du,   You must not
> Was passiert."   speak of this."

They left me there.
Proud backs and crunching heels
Just faded in the woods . . .

That's all I can remember
(still alive at forty-six) . . .
It happened over thirty years
Ago.

—1966

Holocaust

BLOOD
bloodblood
river red
stench grass
green blue grass
bornedown stalks
downoozed night
thunder lipped
flashfar
fire spat
yellow burst
recoil swung
thud flowered
hissoranged
straw crackled
crumble bricked
steel boned
broken snaked
flesh ridged
redblackgray
grime split
mandead
womandead
shriekingdead
stream trickled
purple seeped
sap soaked
open jawed
earth earth earth

Ballad

I feed you
from my cup—o
I feed you
from my cup
which is so
full of gall

I cannot
drink it all

the cup came from my father
he drained it off and mother
refilled it for her son
to taste—her only one

you drink now
of the cup—o
you drink now
of my cup
there is too
bitter gall

for me to
take it all

don't give it to our daughter
pour milk for her or water
our memories are long
but she is still too young

o now you've
broke the cup
this heirloom

of a cup
and spilled
it all

and spilled
the gall

Bars of Dust

Bars of dust would rise
in hymns of resurrection
toward star atoms.

. . . there was shrieking
before the dying
and asphyxiated prayers.

Devils smirked
as they icily calculated
checked-off souls.

Now
those sounds
strain as aeolian echoes
tremulous on the margin
of belief.

Still
I hear them
I to whom revenge
was granted
for the poisoned eyes
of my broken people.

But this justice too
burns lies into
the tongue
for always man
keeps scattering more dust.

Too Everywhere

. . . then I came to the pinched faces,
shriveled ovals with haunted blue rings,
their skull structures too evident;

whose colors proved immaterial
because black, bronze, white and saffron
had gone beach-grey.

mouths, those should-be rose clichés,
flaked parch-pitted phrases
around stunted teeth;

and to speak of their rags
or spine fingers would become obscene.

I could not swallow that night.

Response to a Grand Inquisitor

. . . if you put my feet to the fire,
what will i confess?

What is there left to disclose
in this scalded age?

My obligations to vengeance
are long remitted—

though, prior to *my* Ides of March,
i directed much killing,
without laving my hands
in dramatic madness:
"out! damnéd spot!"

At dawn and dusk
i signaled the approach
of turreted targets:
            location,
            range
            estimated speed,
and telephoned
our mortar elevations
to stop them in their tracks
while crouching under
smoking muzzles.

That was routine . . .

minus the embarrassed value
assigned to body counts—
a practice televised
during a later altercation,
which used up
the bewildered sons
of my veteran generation . . .

My memories have been swathed
in the protective bandages
of telescoped decades.

Only on occasional nights

i still scream

Grisha's Epilogue

After reading *The Testament*, by Elie Wiesel

Draw me a circle, Elijah;
a circle of violated soil,
perfect for the corpses
of many nations.

Let no one escape.
Let the wind carry
millions of moans
to the Unknown One
for His eternal contemplation.

.   .   .   .

I hold secrets
of such enormous presence
that I bit off my tongue
and repudiated sanity.

But inside my skull
the twenty-two symbols
of my ancient alphabet
arrange themselves
into lamentations.

The valley
of the shadow of death
is populated
by expiring sighs.

The world feels still
with a final stillness.

And Elijah,
my messenger-friend,

records the blinking
of the Angel's
numberless eye-lids,
while ravens feed
his candle needs.

. . . . .

I am imprisoned
in the aureole of the circle
and no longer claw
at its sullied walls.

And yet,
and yet:
there rattles in me
sufficient breath
to intone
The Kaddish.

Ultimate Recall

During the last minutes
of my life
I trembled, a naked man,
at the rim of that pit
across which
obscenely grinning gunners
fed fresh belts
into hot barrels.

I was not alone:
hundreds of pallid shapes
shivered,
strung along
blood-steaming clods—
each a death-branded male,
thinking one last defense
of dignity
by covering his shame
with fumbling hands . . .

My reeling nerves
sent loosening signals
to my bowels—
and I stank
before pitching
into final decay.

I will give you a new heart, and will put
a new spirit within you . . . and you shall keep the
statutes, to do them.
                    —Ezekiel 36: 26–27

Not all the bones in the valley
were dry. —To many clung strips
of crimson flesh. Skulls grinned
under matted scalps; curled fingers
grew talons.

The soil had enfolded these innocents
with steaming indifference—
of still pumping veins; the eyes
not quite sight-less
after the grisly rattling
of teeth, of guns,
of gurgling throats.

. . . That proved merely *one* manner
of serving God.

Elsewhere, lethal shower-heads
cleansed life out of
duped victims.
And their bone meal was later reclaimed
for nourishing purpose.

                    ·   ·   ·   ·   ·

Jehovah has not yet breathed
His Spirit
within any of the valley's inmates.
No body has stirred
under His merciful radiance,
or observed His Statutes—

is even this depleted earth
subsiding
into ever more corruption? . . .

Forty Years after Liberation

Where was God's mercy—
where was God? . . .

They died as many deaths
as daemons could devise;
shunted into the stench
of barrack sheols;
savaged by vicious tools
in ghoulish fists;

starved to the marrow;
wasted every hour
until their souls froze
upon blistered lips.

. . . Yet, *we* survived
in the bruised nakedness
of tortured wills.—

There's no forgetting
those seared body heaps
which could not be interred
for lack of earth;
the toxic showers,
the putrid palls of smoke
that shrouded day
and surfeited the night.

. . . . .

When unbelieving troops
broke down the gates,
they retched
at what they saw . . .

then helped us live!

The nightmares stalk us still;
the numbers scar our arms.

We argue
with our God
and question
His Existence—

But *we* exist
and save a stubborn faith
for our children's sake;

and shall bear witness
long beyond the silence
of unknown graves.

3. Ironies

Genesis 37—New Edition

There are no more wells
to cast him into,
though the slavers would again
offer bounty
and lash the rainbowed fool
to fleshpot Egypts . . .

The world has spun off
still another Joseph,
mincing in his prismic robe;
peacock tailed with
a hundred irises,
raised against
a *minyan* of brothers.

Hate churns
inside their frontal lobes;
scorched desert hate,
mumbling like broth—
about to spill
        over
this star stripling's
prancing dream drivel.

Rachel's whelp struts
among the tents,
neither sniffing the
dromedary stench
nor pocketing drovers' curses—
for he loves his own
phrase nights
and girds barmitzvah loins
for a Ra-future . . .

With only Jacob,
that aged angel bouncer,

nodding his shaggy pumpkin;
rattling with the seed faith
of patriarchs.

This son will make it!
He has brains and
a sufficiency of arrogance
to harvest
when improvident tribes
shall lament
drought-bloated kine.
     However,

o farfetched Lord
of the made,
the unmade and
the yet-to-be-made,
sprinkle this youth
with a few grains of
Shem's compassion.

Sectarians

Dispersing
at propitious times
from their
clandestine caverns
they made condolence calls
on the oppressed.

In unseamed robes.

Advancing even
upon cities,
startling sophisticates
some conscience hours
. . . mocked viciously
at the cock's crowing
because of revelations
too grotesque
         . . . though never
by governing beards
who shivered deeply
until the gentle ones
were decently disposed of

by axe or nail

on limbs of blasphemy.

Anathema

Put back your head,
John.
Your executioners died
of bloated morals.

The One Greater than
yourself
expired in good faith,
then rose to glory

and left the rest of the
world
to stink to
high Heaven.

Fragment, Dating Back to the Dark Ages

When I played the biography
of a saint
(there are saints, you know),
I consumed a minimum
and knelt a maximum,
lacing finger bones,
rotating invocations,
urging leather thongs
to mortify instincts
in my blistering anxiety
for the death orgasm
I felt entitled to.

It proved arduous
to make God accept
my worthiness;
and acrid to witness
so many—not at all inclined
toward the martyr's crown—
being raised
because of alien features,
or foreign intonations,
or a special effectiveness
as humans.

. . . In His own time,
of course, the Lord
gazed upon my utterness
of devotion.
And He sanctified
my offenses
against the permanences
with the burning glory
of the heretic's 13 steps.

. . . Having thus been
scattered about the realm
(according to Scripture),
I address you:
mildly warning new zealots
that the sole principle
vouchsafed me from
all the above
terminated in an ikon
for the remainder of Eternity.

York, A. D. 1189

I

The blooming, bluff Plantagenet
affixed the cross;
eager to cast off England;
administering not being chivalrous
and more abrasive to his skull
than crested battle pots.

Still, there was need for cash,
ready to hand.
Sojourns to Holiness
would cost—not in mere body counts,
feudally cheap, but minted marks
eluding the collectors.

> "God's blood! Have We not
> foreigners, richly connected,
> in Our realm?
> Some pressure there
> Should yield a fleet . . ."

Plantagenet weighed consequences:
hard money now . . . prosperity anon.

> "Make them spit gold.
> And—mind you—
> without charge!"

II

Deep in the north's most Norman Keep
they barricaded their integrity,
mulcted of coin,
cornered by Richard's poor.

Some earls,
less zealous than the Lionheart,
held back the pious for a day—
vomited titled shame
and finally departed
to chastise infidels on Zion's plains.

Prayerful elders
drew the sacred knives:
Three generations bled
unaided, undefiled
before the gates were breached . . . .

Had They Been There

I

Might Mozart have
attempted some feeble
jest while his
fingertips bruised those
reeking floor boards
with adagio dots
of pity . . . would
he have traced
a martyr's cross
against helmeted herders
whose Ninth Circle
moved, inexorably freezing,
toward their loins?

II

Would Beethoven have
blasphemed in thematic
defiance at the
Übermensch banality of
clicking heels . . . might
he have hummed
a Marche Funêore
and—would he
finally stomp, head
thrust forward, hands
behind his back,
to drum four
staccato notes on
the wall of
a fuming shower? . . .

Sermon from the Ammunition Hatch of the Ship of Fools

Armored again ride the Ages,
and dark.
Dark like unlit silos, brimming with
lurching seas of grain one
can drown in, being trapped.
Dark like monsoon trails under
exotic greens, crackling
death.
Dark like *no* skin, though
pale Burden-bearers still expand
upon their singularity.
Dark in the hotels of learning from
Sacramento to Peiping.

. . . in my boy-days, shirts
goose-stepped in serried brown. My
middle years (after t/rifled victories)
sport narrow-drab trousers or
—more revealing—the
primary tonalities of
flap-tailed tourists. HATE
splinters slum glass, isolated
by cameras of courage.
The ghettos stink on front pages in
black. Cities gangrene like
wounded comrades, jettisoned to
save a retreat.

And we circle the dark of the moon by
technical proxy; but our
murderers face faces in the sun.—
Armored again ride the Ages, and, God,
DAMNED DARK!

Miserabile

Deciphering your black skin
with my jewish whiteness
i begin to sweat

sweat blood
crimson as yours
as Cherokees'
Navajos'

both more original
on this continent
than you or me

sweat shame
underdog shame
victim excrescence
remembering
my six million kin
obliterated

. . . you and i are
lucky
in a way
having survived
to testify

and:
i seem to have
made it—
but for how long?
considering
my
two hundred
hunted-down decades . . .

it's your turn
to be leavened

that's what
i'd like to promise
without shamming
just hoping
that
"justice shall (will) prevail."

Here is where the words stop
stop—across the world

the truth has
a total solution:
all colors are to melt
in the next holocaust.

4. Witness

Preface

I am the stranger
truly not alien
to man nor wordlife
yet a notborn
american
far from—

With only phrase roots
the hebrew's
native tendrils
in everwhich soil
german
by cosmic joke
so happened . . .

But how
can any speech
drumming
immigrant ears
escape fingers
compulsive
across space
if feeling counts
mock
every else act?

Maimonides

The Tzadik lives on a smile;
a hesitant arch—
like a fern
at noon,
or like the
devout shoulders
of a quiet benediction.

Spinoza

Now you
circle Substance
in your sweep
nearer the stars.

Some lake below
an aquamarine leaf
of quietude
reflects
an eagle shadow.

We scan it
between
snow pyramids
through your
illusion
of God.

Franz Kafka

i claw into myself—
i, visceral judge,
grave-edged,
hunger-sated.

The castle crumbles
against the
ear-shell
of my begging.

Executioners,
after screw-driving
with daggers,
sew me
into guilt.

And—quite outside
my red-rimmed,
time-wired husk—
i laugh
predestined laughs
at insect parodies.

Albert Camus

Curtained by the ramparts
Of this I,
This self-inflicted oneness
Not tied to any else—
Yet sensing similarities
Grope past,
Halt for a phrase
To share their mankindness
And shuffle into limbo—

You are. They are.
Walled tensely in one city,
Concrete in need,
Each of the other,
To cleanse the charnel house
Of pustulent effusions,
Of busy-bodied dying rats
That scurry through
The yellow-gray decay—

You shall; they might
Resist the terror-oozing plague
With calmly measured
Decencies of hope.

Refugee Memoir

Since over me the Origins hung shadows
black as a lacquered lake in Brandenburg
beneath pine helmets;
since through my veins such currents tide—
likely from deltas—cold by half, half geyser-hot;
since I remember in my childhood landscape
provincial castle and a gallows hill
and two-track railroad—
    I grow painfully
much like persistent ivy on neglected graves.

Like it I need to cover nakedness
and leaden parsimony,
and a past,
for blood has bled too copiously loud
before my windows:
Nostrils have memories . . .

No nostalgia that—
from five to twenty-five!—
So many hands retracted into fists,
while drumming race-lust froze the coughing lungs
with kicking Lugers
until a visa drafted me to dignity.

And later: crawling through the muck
of beachheads raped by necessary hate,
I fire-ordered death and loved the man
in me . . .
but could not curse compassion . . . .

Journey to Orcus

My head turns in all directions;
alternately up and down
like an apple in the wind—
or sideways
with a pine cone scaliness.

Occasionally,
it stares silently
toward where the dead
stubbornly decompose.
And (quite rarely)
it challenges the sun
with the inanest urge
—to smile.

My head stands gray now,
snow aged,
in the world's shocks,
of its two hundred
conscious seasons.

All the wisdom it shells
is reducible
to an equation
of falling bodies . . .

Still,
my knuckles keep testing
stalactites
down stygian grottoes;
the eyes swimming about
on the exhaustion of my legs.

Every sense breath sears
with rifled impact
while the cavern grows

a winding sheet
around my freezing flesh.

I grope against satans
who whisper
through draining wall crusts
archaic Eden accusations—
to be repeated—
touch by touch.

It is no better above:
the sun hangs hooded,
mourning earth's corpsing.

My wick gutters . . .

I cannot stop filling
a fallen angel's skin.

Nelly Sachs

what shall one say to a sister
whose comprehensions blade-flame
from stoic pages—
still splitting dreams?
what does one mail to her
from a distant dawn
where palm and oak
cohabit illusions of the sun?
. . . that i too escaped
those cross-hooked standards;
that my carbine cracked the lives
of once countrymen?
that in myself too
everything congeals
—sobs and jubilations—
into love-inventing lines? . . .

April 5, 1968—
Martin Luther King

in sudden recognition
the nation lowered
its proud flags

the breast-beating
was audible
around the globe

white faces grieved
against black shoulders
scalded with guilt

because the courage
of one man
had entered peace

April 6, 1968

Lament for Paul Celan
(1920–1970)

and—
had i not suffered the ice-anguish
or the candle-pain of your past,
i should have scorned
your calculated steps
into hereafters—

when you might have chanted
yet further praise and prayers
of the damned—
in guilt-creations,
for being meant to borrow life
when kindred fragments
were showered to filthy deaths
or scratched out
on their battle fields.

        . . . . .

How did i manage
to move in present/futures;
to function—however tensely—
within corruption?

—i, given up
as totally unfleshed
upon a bogged-down beachhead?

i do not know . . .

Having signed a truce
with trigger-short existence,
i keep the record of my sorrow
for all

whose threads of innocence
were severed
as testimony to the banal aberrations,
fashioned in God's Likeness . . . .

Pablo Neruda

Many gutters have
run red threads
through betrayed cities.

Many trees were
hung with crops
so ripe they
could not fall.

O Santiago, you
too suffered the
staccato pitting of
white proud facades:

But your poet
has already seeded
his father's land.

"The Gates of the Forest"

cannot be unlocked
by philistines.

No path is marked
to guide those souls
that chose to forget.

Of precise memory
the messengers only
decipher the trail

Where innocents bled
to trace the hem
of Gabriel.

Encounter

Descending from Judea's hills
he ruffled his beard
with defiant fingers
and smoothed the
temptation-saturated robe.

i ascended from the valleys.

and we met.

"shalom" he saluted.
"shalom" i replied.

"are you one of my people?"

"I don't know.
your people have made matters
difficult for mine
since you acquired
those perforations."

his mouth tautened:
"they are not my people!"

no. they really are not.

he and i shared the longing
of Israel's eyes—
both fishermen
with words for nets.

we might have become friends
despite the centuries
that made him into god
and me into ashes . . . .

5. Resurgence

Summary

it had to be so,
has to be so—
the wind is neutral,
but vicious
as the scavengers
of men
in our memory . . .

when those of us,
who seek,
play the stars
like David—
questions fume
in vapors
from our minds
until frost
ages
our shoulders.

the soul,
the hoped-for
permanence,
hovers about,
not settling
on anyone;
not becoming an answer.

we cannot
shed tears;
we dare not shake
with laughter.
life is
the shrug
to our knowledge;

and we find
strength
to move on.

Anniversary—October, 1965

Twenty years
sum up
an honorable
span.

The War
having massacred
our past,
we needed life;

So our histories mingled.

And since
our dreams
had not been
also murdered,

We seeded
them
with yet a
generation.

Hasidic Dance

Ecstatic
gabardine wings
spread against
ceilinged heaven.

Every shabbat-
eased scar
expands under
guttering tallow
into a rafterless
essence.

Ringlets and
whiskers leap
their own
most intricate figures
glossy with
vaunted release.

Plangent tonalities
surge
through sensuous
cabalist maelstroms.

Laughter-heavy
each I
achieving the
ambient Thou.

The Denmark Square Monument
in Jerusalem

Blesséd those small,
unlighted vessels
which smuggled the condemned
out of the executioner's reach.

More blesséd still
their crews,
compassionately scornful
of the master race.

Most blesséd the nation
that sewed yellow stars
upon its sleeves
to face down swastikas.

They were indomitable.

And when I stood
before the symbol ship—
iron as Danish courage—
I thought of my father

Who was a gentle branch
of that glorious tree.

Memorandum

i have been drilled
in survival
by circumstance

>death had a hand
in that—
tendering his
stygian cloak
as a forever
anesthetic
(at least twice
reeking
of cordite)
desisting solely
because my puissance
wrenched free
at the crucial
instants

for: i had marked
too many
spun into
perdition
without a cry
of battle

>or relinquishing
their grip
second
by
malignant
second

most of them
worthy

to complete
their missions

ALL TIME (I HAVE
OBSERVED) IS
HOUR-
GLASSED . . . AND
WEIGHED AGAINST ME

i shall not
therefore
squander it
with any labor
less than

LOVE

The Chagall Windows

o the fires!
           orange fierceness
           crimson bloom

o the seas!
           beryl surf
           cobalt foam

o the creatures!
           Wingéd
           horn-tipped
           multi-hued
           like Joseph's robes

o the yield of Canaan!
           strewn across
           the glass expanse
           of jeweled tribes

o the light upon our souls!
           born of sun
           and genius

o the AMEN to our kind!

Chai

Now the oak looms
in its tallith
of ochre leaves
against the dun
of hollow skies.

Many a tree
has withered thus.

We stand as
witnesses to
transitions
and mourn—
each from the depths
of our reasons.

Still, we remain
children
toward the future
and shall,
even as this oak
commemorate
the destiny
of our covenant
with foliage renewed.

6. *Translations*

from Nelly Sachs's Journey into a Dustless Realm

Nelly Sachs is a religious poet, a delineator of the mysteries of deep distress and possible salvation. Only the iron patience of faith can keep this spirit alive or permit the body to accept death.

In 1940 she was saved from the Nazi executioner by the intervention of Sweden's great novelist Selma Lagerlöff (who had received the Nobel Prize in 1909 for *Gösta Berling*).

Twenty-six years later, Nelly Sachs's poems—"dipped in fire"— struck the world which was about to forget the long agony of the thirties and the Second World War, and stood armed for the new generation's bloodletting.

Journey into a Dustless Realm (Frankfurt am Main: Suhrkamp Verlag, 1961) reminds us of inferno and warns against the New Cruelty already in progress. These poems are so unique that they express the universal. One individual's perception has found the words that all people must accept. Suffering and overcoming walk hand in hand as did mother and child at Belsen, Buchenwald, and Auschwitz. Human beings, caught in the web of their frustration, can destroy the mold but not the *nous*— the essence—of their fellows. And, like the outward form of this being, Nelly Sachs's work is shaped with a balance, rhythm, and imagery that reveal the striving for continuance of the spirit.

Miss Sachs was not an idle optimist. Yet, she burns hope into our minds—perhaps into our hearts as well—as only a great poet can.

I shared with Nelly Sachs the tragic experiences of Germany's dishonor. I later fought my former countrymen as an American soldier. Perhaps this gives me the right to translate her threnodies.

The page numbers refer to the 1961 German edition, which I translated in 1966.

Untitled

P. 11

But who emptied the sand from your shoes
When you had to arise to meet death?
That sand which Israel carried home,
His journey-gathered sand?
The burning Sinai-sand,
Wed to nightingale throats,
The wings of butterflies
And the serpent's longing dust—
Fused with whatever was shed by Solomon's wisdom
With the wormwood's secrets.

O ye fingers
That emptied the sand from the shoes of the dead—
Ye shall be the dust of tomorrow
Filling the shoes of the future!

A Dead Child Speaks

P. 13

Mother held my hand.
Then someone raised the knife of separation:
Mother withdrew her hand
That the blade would not strike me.
But softly she touched my hip once more—
And her hand was bleeding.

From that instant the parting blade
Cut the morsel in my throat—
At dawn it glistened with the sun
And began to sharpen within my eyes—
Whetted wind and water rang in my ear
And every voice of comfort pierced my heart.

When I was led unto death
I felt, that last moment,
The withdrawing of the great, severing knife.

Chorus of Stars

PP. 60-61

We are the stars:
Wandering, glowing, singing dust—
Our sister, the earth, has been struck blind
Among the lustrous images of heaven.
She has become an outcry
Among them who chant—
She, most steeped in yearning;
Who from dust began her labor: to mold angels—
Who, deep within her mystery, bears bliss
Like gold-silted streams—
Now, like wine poured out upon the night,
Pooled in forsaken alleys—
Upon her substance flickers the saffron
                              phosphorescence of evil.

Earth, oh earth,
Star of stars,
Gridded with the threads of longing,
God-begun—
Is no one left to recall your youth?
No one to immolate himself in the seas of death?
Has no man's desire ripened
To rise like the angel-winged seed
Of the dandelion's calix?

Earth, earth, have you gone blind
Before the Pleiades' sisterly eyes
Or Libra's probing gaze?

Murderous hands have proffered Israel a mirror
Wherein—dying—it could view its death—

Earth, oh earth,
Star of stars—
Someday one galaxy will be named Mirror.
Then, blind one, shall you see again.

Chorus of the Clouds

P. 63

We are heavy with sighs, full of glances,
Replete with laughter.
And sometimes we bear your faces.
Nor are we far removed . . .
Who knows how much of your ascending blood
Has colored us?
Who knows how many of your tears
Have issued from our weeping—
How much yearning has shaped us?
We are partners in the game of Death,
And gently accustom you to him;
You, who remain untested and learn nothing
                                    in the nights.
Many angels are given you,
But you do not see them.

Untitled

P. 143

Like flames, at times, it surges
through our bodies—
as if they were to be woven
into the Alpha of the stars.

How tardily we alight unto clarity—

O, after how many light years
have our hands braided supplication—
have our knees genuflected—
have our souls opened
toward gratitude?

Untitled

P. 161

Ebb and tide play one chord,
hunter and hunted.
Countless hands attempt
to grasp, to fortify—
The thread is blood

Fingers trace dispositions
limbs strain out from
expiring drawings

Strategy—
the odor of suffering—

Limb-iotas on their way to dust
and the foam of longing
upon the waters

Untitled

When lightning
struck the edifice of faith,
feet traversed the waters
and arms echoed, wing-spread, in the air

Only melancholy—
that wine distilled
for grave-stone angels
who shall at last sleep a sufficiency—
flowed back to earth

Chassidic Dance

P. 198

Night stirs with banners
torn from death.

Hats of black,
God's lightning rods,
goad the sea,

weigh it,
measure it out

and cast it upon the shore
where light has excised
those black wounds.

The whole world is savored
on the tongue
and, breathed with
hereafter-lungs,
is chanted out.

And the Pleiades pray
on the menorah's
seven prongs.

Untitled

P. 205

With his star tracings
Daniel arose
from the crags in Israel . . .
Where time found its death-home,
there arose Daniel,
the angels' gatherer of shards—
the preserver of shredded things
to fix the last fulcrum
between beginning and end.

Daniel, who quarries unremembered dreams
from that final anthracite-seeded slope.

Daniel, who instructed Belshazzar in the
deciphering of blood,
that script of lost wound-ridges
fire-caught.

Daniel, who tapped his way through the
tear-flooded labyrinth
between slayer and slain.

Daniel lifts his finger
out of Israel's twilight.

Untitled

P. 386

So lonely is man
that he searches toward the east
where woe arises
in the twilight countenance.

Red glows the east
from the cock's crowing.

O hear me—

To perish
in leonine cravings
and the lashing bolts
of the equator.

O hear me—

To wilt with cherubic infant faces
at evening.

O hear me—
To wake in the night
on the blue north of the
compass-rose,
a petal of death
already upon the lids

and thus on toward the source—

photo by Eva Durann

ABOUT THE AUTHOR

Hans Juergensen is a professor of humanities at the University of South Florida and the author of fifteen books of poetry. His poems have appeared in many anthologies and periodicals, including the *New York Times, Hopkins Review,* and *Poet Lore.* He has received the Hart Crane—Alice Williams Foundation Award and, twice, the Stephen Vincent Benét Narrative Poetry Award. From 1976 to 1980 he served as consultant to the Nobel Prize Committee on Literature. He was named Florida poet of the year in 1965, 1968, and 1974.